TWELVE
Women
OF THE BIBLE

LIFE-CHANGING STORIES
FOR WOMEN TODAY

STUDY GUIDE
by Sherry Harney

TWELVE

Women

OF THE BIBLE

LIFE-CHANGING STORIES
FOR WOMEN TODAY

12 SESSIONS

Based on teaching from:

LYSA TERKEURST and
ELISA MORGAN, JEANNE STEVENS, AMENA
BROWN, NAOMI ZACHARIAS, JONALYN FINCHER

ZONDERVAN®

ZONDERVAN

Twelve Women of the Bible Study Guide

Real Women, Real Faith: Volume 1 Participant's Guide
Copyright © 2010 by Sherry Harney

Real Women, Real Faith: Volume 2 Participant's Guide
Copyright © 2010 by Sherry Harney

This title is also available as a Zondervan ebook.

Requests for information should be addressed to:
Zondervan, 3900 *Sparks Dr. SE, Grand Rapids, Michigan 49546*

ISBN 978-0-310-08826-4

Cover design: Rob Monacelli
Cover photography: Yuri Arcurs / Getty Images
Interior design: Ben Fetterley and Scribe Inc.

First printing December 2016 / Printed in the United States of America

CONTENTS

INTRODUCTION

Let's Get Real!

Don't you just love authentic people? Aren't you drawn to women who are transparent and real? There is something fresh and wonderful about women who have nothing to hide and who are not ashamed about who they are . . . even the tough parts.

Real faith calls a woman to be honest about who she is. The truth is, God knows everything about us and he loves us beyond description! He knows our strengths, joys, and victories. God also knows our frailties, struggles, sins, and brokenness. In the midst of all of this, he is crazy about us.

When we get this truth, and this truth gets a grip on our hearts, everything changes. Like the Velveteen Rabbit in the classic children's story, we slowly become "Real." We don't have to hide from God and each other. We can admit our struggles and celebrate our joys.

We can become real women with real faith!

In this twelve-session small group journey you will meet a group of amazing women who are absolutely real. At moments you might wonder why God captured these particular stories in the pages of his Holy Word. But, as you press on, you will discover that the raw and revealing accounts are a gift to women today.

Their stories are not fairytales, their road was not easy, and their examples are not perfect. They lived in times and places quite different than ours. Yet they teach us lessons that are deeply practical, holding up a mirror to our lives and souls that can help us better understand our own story.

As you meet these real women, open your heart to what God wants to do in you. He invites you to come to him as you are, with total transparency. He also wants you to be honest with the women in your small group. If there was ever a time to be honest about who you are . . . it is now. If there was ever a safe place to share your heart and story with humble authenticity, it is in this group.

May God bless your time together and may you become real, before God, yourself, and the women in your small group.

EVE

**FINDING LASTING CONTENTMENT
IN THE TRUTH**

Key Scriptures: Genesis 1:31;
2:15–25; 3:1–7; and
Matthew 4:1–11

Lysa TerKeurst

MEETING EVE

Eve's life began as a study in perfection. She had the dream and then some! Perfect surroundings. Perfect relationships. Perfect provision. And Eve experienced perfect communion with the living God. What more could anyone long for?

Eve's life was a series of "firsts" in the history of the world. She was the first woman, the first wife, the first mother, the first (and only) sinless woman, and the first to be tempted by Satan. Sadly, Eve was the first (along with her husband Adam) to fall into sin and see the cataclysmic consequences of disobedience to God.

Her very name meant, "mother of all who have life," but her story was a tapestry woven with joy and pain, celebration and sorrow, life and death. Eve feasted on the glory of intimacy with God beyond what any other woman would know on the earth. But she also felt her teeth put on edge by the bitter poison of sin and rebellion.

Never has another woman lived with such highs and lows. From the sinless paradise of Eden to the barrenness of exile outside of the garden, angels posted to make sure she and her husband would never return and eat from the tree of life. From perfect communion with Adam and God to the naked shame of being caught in sin. From peaceful relationships to the unspeakable pain that came as she stood over the grave of a son who had been murdered by his own brother. Eve knew the whole spectrum of human emotion.

Eve was swept into the spiritual drama that would unfold through the whole story of the human family and the Word of God. She was molded and shaped by the very hands of God and had no earthly parents. She faced the tempter and heard his sinister voice entice her to rebel against God. She heard the prophetic word that one day Satan would be crushed by her ancestor:

> "I will put enmity between you and the woman,
>   and between your offspring and hers;
>   he will crush your head, and you will strike his heel."

> Genesis 3:15

Eve saw the cost of sin but heard the message of hope in a coming Savior, one who would be her descendant. His name would be Jesus!

Introduction

The more things change, the more they stay the same!

Just think about it. Every mother from the dawn of time has had to teach her children to say two simple words, "Thank you." If every mom had a dollar for every time they said to a son or daughter, "What do you say?" every mom would be a millionaire! Some things never change.

Every Christian woman, from the first century on, has longed to have a little more time to pray, read the Word, and sit at the feet of Jesus. But our lives get so busy and cluttered it can be difficult. Some things are just part of our lot as human beings. The more things change, the more they really do stay the same.

That is what we will learn in today's session about Eve. She was tempted and enticed by the enemy, just as we all are. Satan's tactics were calculated, strategic, and effective. When we watch Eve's drama unfold, we see that the same tactics the devil used against her were used against Jesus when he walked on this earth. With this in mind, we should expect the enemy to use similar wiles and schemes against us. Because, the more things change, the more they stay the same.

As you enter into this session, open your ears and heart. Prepare yourself to learn about the tactics of the enemy and ask God to prepare you to fight back. The same deceiving schemer that slithered up to Eve in the garden and Jesus in the desert is still looking to entice people to follow his lies and turn from the ways of Jesus. In this small group gathering you will be fortified to identify his tactics and fight back. This is extremely important and practical stuff that the devil does not want you to hear. But God has brought you to this moment because he has a message just for you.

Talk About It

Briefly respond as a group to one of the following questions.

Tell a brief story about a "first" in your life:

- First date
- First meal you cooked
- First time driving
- Any first . . .

Sometimes in life we have high hopes and big expectations, but things just don't turn out the way we had imagined and dreamed. Tell about one such time in your life.

"Sometimes we miss the miraculous of all that we have been blessed with because we're so focused on the one thing we don't have. When this happens, we become disillusioned with all that we do have."

Lysa TerKeurst

Video Teaching Notes

The temptation to focus on the one thing we don't have

Three ways Eve was tempted and consumed:

Physical pleasure

Material possessions

Desire for significance

How Satan tempts women today

Danger sign: when we want the things of this world more than the will of God

The temptation of Jesus

Jesus' solution: "It is written"

Back up and look up: worshiping only God

Philippians 4:6–7

"The Lord is near!"

"The next time the cup of your heart feels a little empty, remember to step back and look up and realize that nothing in this world can fill the cup of your heart. . . . Let God fill your cup."
Lysa TerKeurst

Small Group Study and Video Discussion

1. **Read:** Genesis 1:31 and 2:15–25. Lysa points out that Adam and Eve had perfect surroundings, perfect relationships, and perfect provision—all of their needs met by God's loving care. Yet they still wanted more. They gave in to temptation and fed the desire for what they did not have . . . or need! How do you see this in our world and culture today? How do you decide the difference between your wants and needs?

2. For Adam and Eve, the one thing they were not supposed to fixate on and desire was a specific tree in the garden. What are some things that people can be lured to focus on in our world that are not healthy or meant to be the center of our attention and lives?

3. **Read:** Genesis 3:1–7. What specific tactics did Satan use to lure Eve into sin and how does he use these same strategies today?

4. **Read:** 1 John 2:15–17. John addresses the same three temptation points that Satan used against Eve: the cravings of sinful man (physical pleasure), the lust of his eyes (materialism), and the boasting of what we have and do (significance). In the video, Lysa reminds us of the danger of holding out the cup of our heart and letting it be filled with things that do not honor God or fully satisfy our desires. Which of these three areas of temptation is the enemy's greatest lure against you and how do you seek to fight against it?

5. **Read:** Matthew 4:1–11. How did Jesus respond when the enemy tried to tempt him and what do you learn from Jesus' response?

6. Lysa uses a line, "Back up and look up." What is she encouraging us to do when we are faced by the sinister temptation of the enemy? How can we do this?

7. As you back up and look up in the midst of one of the areas of temptation you are struggling with at this time in life, what Bible passage(s) could fortify and strengthen you?

In what ways might you keep this passage and biblical truth in the forefront of your mind, and how can your group members keep you accountable to back up and look up as you face this temptation?

"When you find yourself being tempted, learn from Jesus. . . . He immediately took his eyes off the temptation and puts them on to God's Word."

Lysa TerKeurst

8. What hope do you receive when you remind yourself that "the Lord is near"?

When you feel like the cup of your heart is empty, how do you go about filling it up?

"Do not be anxious about anything, but in every situation, by prayer and petition, with thanksgiving, present your requests to God. And the peace of God, which transcends all understanding, will guard your hearts and your minds in Christ Jesus."

Philippians 4:6–7

Group Prayer Direction

- Thank God for his Word and the power it brings to our lives. Thank Jesus for his example of battling the enemy with the words of Scripture. Thank the Holy Spirit for the times he brings the truth of Scripture to your mind when the enemy is near.
- Ask God to help you fall in love with his Word and feed on it daily so you are fortified and equipped for the attacks Satan will bring against you.
- Surrender the areas of your life where you are facing temptation.
- One sign that temptation is coming is when we start focusing on what we *don't* have. One remedy to this problem is to celebrate the good things we *do* have. Take time to thank God for the good gifts he has given you.
- Ask God to help you to, "Be anxious about nothing, but in everything, by prayer and petition, with thanksgiving, present your requests to God" (Philippians 4:6). Pray that his peace will cover your life, fill your heart, and guide your days.

Journal Between Sessions

What are some of the daily miracles you might miss if you let yourself focus too much on what you don't have? Give thanks to God for your daily miracles as you list them.

_____

_____

_____

_____

_____

_____

_____

_____

_____

_____

_____

_____

_____

_____

_____

_____

_____

REBEKAH

BREAKING FREE OF FEMININE STEREOTYPES

Key Scriptures: Genesis 24 and 25:19–34

Jonalyn Fincher

MEETING REBEKAH

Rebekah was a strong woman . . . in virtually every way possible! She was a picture of feminine strength. When we first meet her in the biblical narrative she offers to bring water for ten thirsty camels. This task would have taken a considerable amount of time drawing and pouring, a sign of her physical strength and endurance. Rebekah had intellectual strength as well. She had a sharp mind and the ability to recognize and respond to what was happening around her. She had great emotional strength. Rebekah was courageous. When she was asked to pack up her belongings and travel a great distance to begin a new life with a man named Isaac, she was ready to go! Finally, she had spiritual fortitude. Rebekah walked with a great measure of faith and trust in God . . . even when she did not know what the future held.

Like so many of us, Rebekah was also a person of paradox. Mingled in with her strengths were points of weakness. The mother of twins, Jacob and Esau, she got pulled into the dangerous practice of playing favorites with them. She trusted God in some situations, but she was not above manipulating people to get what she wanted. Motherhood came late for Rebekah. For the first twenty years of her married life, she was barren, even though God had made a covenant with Abraham and promised that his descendants would be as many as the sands on the seashore. Rebekah was aware of God's promise, and yet she lived with her broken dreams—childless for two decades—until the twins came! Rebekah deeply loved her husband and her sons, but we learn that she also had a shadow side. At one point in her life, Rebekah deliberately deceived two of those closest to her: Esau and Isaac. Her ambitious dreams for her "favorite" son strained her marriage, lost her the esteem of her oldest son, and eventually led to the loss of her favored son, Jacob, who was forced to flee town to escape his brother's anger, fearful for his life.

When we peek behind the curtain of Rebekah's life we find a real woman, not a simplistic stereotype. Rebekah doesn't fit into neat little categories—and neither can you or I! To get to know Rebekah and learn to be honest about ourselves we will need to break free from some of the common feminine stereotypes and come humbly to God . . . just as we are.

Introduction

Stereotypes, labels, and boxes . . . they make life so much easier. Let's be honest, when we are not careful and attentive, we can all slip into this habit. We just slap on a label, put a person in our little box, or use a broad stereotype and we don't have to deal with who they really are.

So what does it mean to be a godly woman? A whole list of feminine stereotypes likely come to mind, descriptions that are often used with little thought or reflection. But when we meet Rebekah, she shatters some of the simplistic boxes we like to put women into. Rebekah was one of the matriarchs of the faith and is in the bloodline of King David . . . and Jesus himself.

At first, Rebekah seems to line up with some of the more traditional stereotypes. She is quiet, humble, and willing to serve.

But then, we discover that she is articulate, has strong opinions, and is ready to speak her mind. She is bold and courageous. Those are qualities that stretch some of the more traditional feminine stereotypes.

Sadly, we also discover that Rebekah can be deceptive, manipulative, and downright controlling. How does this fit with our simple categories for women of faith? Why would God use a sinful woman like Rebekah in his redemptive story? Rebekah was a stereotype-breaking, box-shattering, label-confounding woman of God, and her strengths and frailties are laid bare before us in Scripture.

The truth is that, like Rebekah, we all are women of great strength and profound weaknesses. Rather than glossing over our failures and trying to fit our lives into a predefined understanding of what makes a godly woman, the story of Rebekah teaches us that God uses all kinds of women to accomplish his purposes. None of us fit the stereotype, if we are willing to take an honest look at who God has made us to be.

Talk About It

Briefly respond as a group to one of the following questions.

What are some of the stereotypes of women that culture promotes these days?

What characteristic and qualities mark the life of a courageous woman?

"God isn't limited to use a certain type of woman with a certain list of characteristics. . . . He loves using variety."

Jonalyn Fincher

Video Teaching Notes

Rebekah is not a typical feminine woman

Abraham's prayerful servant finds a wife for Isaac in Rebekah

Abraham's journey in comparison to Rebekah's

The mother of Jacob and Esau

Rebekah's life is not perfect and she is not a "perfect woman"

And yet God uses her: matriarch in the bloodline of Jesus

How Rebekah's courage can remind us of Jesus

The struggle to feel comfortable with our own bodies (breaking feminine stereotypes)

You are wonderfully made

"The same strengths that we see God using to prepare Rebekah to be the wife of Isaac also end up wounding her family and herself, and yet God uses her."

Jonalyn Fincher

Small Group Study and Video Discussion

1. **Read:** Genesis 24. What characteristics do you admire in Rebekah as you meet her in this passage?

How do the characteristics you see in Rebekah line up or go against the grain of traditional views of what it means to be feminine?

2. What are some of the similarities between Rebekah and her eventual father-in-law, Abraham?

3. **Read:** Genesis 25:19–34. Jonalyn makes the observation that Rebekah's strengths also had a shadow side. Her quick mind that allowed her to respond to the servant of Abraham early in her story was also the same mind that allowed her to concoct a plan to help her favorite son, Jacob, steal his brother's birthright. Consider some of your own strengths. How might an area of strength also have a "shadow side" and become dangerous if you are not careful?

4. **Read:** John 13:2–5; 13–17. How is Rebekah's example of humble service similar to Jesus' willingness to wash his disciples' feet? How do you see a Christlike spirit in Rebekah?

5. Jonalyn says, "Women who are courageous are comfortable in their own skin." What does a woman who is comfortable in her own skin look like?

What does it look like when a woman is not comfortable in her own skin?

"If femininity is worth its salt, it cannot be bought and sold; femininity will be something you already are, not something you have to become."

Jonalyn Fincher

6. If you were sitting with Jonalyn over a cup of tea and she asked you, "When did the bad relationship between you and your body begin?" what would you tell her?

7. Name some of the sources of input that define beauty in our culture and help shape our view of our own body and sense of beauty. Why do you think we give these sources such authority over us?

"Women who are courageous are women who are comfortable in their own skin. They know their own strengths, they know what they offer, they know what their bodies can give, they know their limitations, they know the strength of their soul; they are comfortable in who they are."

Jonalyn Fincher

8. **Read:** Psalm 139:13–14. Jonalyn teaches that certain things about your body are unique and a blessing from God. What is some aspect of your body that you are thankful for and that God uses for his glory?

"I am fearfully and wonderfully made; your works are wonderful, I know that full well."

Psalm 139:14

Group Prayer Direction

- Invite God into your struggle of accepting those things that he has uniquely given you in your body that you have not been particularly thankful for.
- Pray for the women in your group to be freed from stereotypes, boxes, and labels that have sought to define them.
- Pray that each woman would become the woman of God she is destined to be and inspire others to do the same.
- As we learned from Rebekah, our strengths can have shadow sides. Pray that God would reveal anything in us that might be leading us to act in ungodly ways.
- Thank God for the women God has placed in your life to influence and lead you. Praise God for the ways they have moved beyond limiting stereotypes into freedom to live for him.

Journal Between Sessions

Jonalyn stated: "There are certain things about your body and your soul that are unique and make you stand out. There are certain things that make people notice you when you walk into a room. These might even be the things you don't like about yourself. Sometimes they are the hardest things to own. It can be hard to say that God made me this way on purpose." Journal about these things . . . and if you dare, lift up a prayer of thanks for something about yourself that you have wondered, "God, why did you make me this way?"

_____

_____

_____

_____

_____

_____

_____

_____

_____

_____

_____

_____

_____

LEAH

OVERCOMING REJECTION
AND INSECURITY

Key Scriptures: Genesis 29
and 30:1–24

Naomi Zacharias

MEETING LEAH

The Bible says that Leah had "weak eyes." This either meant that Leah's eyesight was hindered or that her eyes lacked the sparkle that some of the other more attractive women had . . . women like her little sister, Rachel. Through the years Leah had become painfully aware of her unattractiveness. It would be comforting to think that society's obsession with physical appearance was a recent invention, but women have had to deal with this since the beginning of time!

Leah's life journey included not only the pain of feeling unattractive, but consistent rejection by the man she loved. Though she bore Jacob six sons and one daughter, she seemed to always feel like a second-rate citizen, even in her own home. When we read her story we can feel the pain oozing from her soul.

Leah's and Rachel's rivalry ended up bringing tension to their home and luring in the people around them. Yet in the midst of this family civil war, God showed up and cared for Leah. God saw her pain, was near her, and blessed her.

Leah's story captures the depths of sorrow, heartache, and longing. But it also reminds us that God is present and working in our lives in ways we may not see this side of eternity. Though her life was filled with times of sadness, Leah also bore the first son to Jacob, one of the patriarchs of the faith. She was the mother of many of his children. And Leah carried on the bloodline that would one day lead to King David and finally to the Messiah and Lord of all, Jesus!

Introduction

Do you remember the classic story of the Ugly Duckling? This little duck just does not fit in. She's different, gangly, and unattractive . . . and the other little ducks don't accept her.

You probably know how the story ends, though. We learn that the "ugly" duckling was really not a duckling at all, but a baby swan! By the end of the story she has grown into a majestic and beautiful creature, much more attractive than all the ducks that had looked down on her. And like most children's stories, she lives "happily ever after," the envy of the other birds.

Leah's story is not quite as simple and sweet. As we peer into Leah's heart, we learn the hard truth that some journeys don't have "happy" endings. They are difficult from start to finish. Leah walked a painful path in her life, but God was still with her. From what we can tell, her husband never seemed to cherish her, but we know that God loved her with a passion. She never became the stunning swan in the eyes of the world or the eyes of her husband, but she was beautiful in the eyes of her heavenly Father. And she was given the great honor of continuing the bloodline of God's Messiah. One day, her descendant Jesus Christ would show the world the full measure of God's amazing love.

In today's session we will be invited to look beneath the surface of our lives—no matter how difficult and hard they may seem—and discover that the same God who saw, loved, and blessed Leah is ready to do the same for you.

Talk About It

Briefly respond as a group to one of the following questions.

What is a story with a "happily ever after" ending that you enjoyed during your childhood? What about this story drew you in?

What life lesson have you learned from a woman who has walked through a tragedy and held the hand of Jesus along the way?

> *"The value and the beauty of every story is not always found in the ending, but sometimes in the very fight itself."*
>
> **Naomi Zacharias**

Video Teaching Notes

Leah's story: a life of hurt and rejection

Mark of distinction for Leah: the unloved wife

Milestones in Leah's faith journey

God saw Leah

God blessed Leah

God loved Leah

God remembered Leah

The names of children and their significance in the story

Gems for life

Blessings in the midst of Leah's pain

The promise of redemption, salvation, and hope for the world came through the descendants of Leah

The place of beauty and a true legacy

> *"Some battles, like so many in life, are not ones that are fought in a single occasion. Some battles have to be fought for the rest of our lives. Some battles have to be fought again and again . . . this is the playground of real life."*
>
> **Naomi Zacharias**

Small Group Study and Video Discussion

1. **Read:** Genesis 29:16–30. What do you learn from the passage about each of the main characters in this story?

   Jacob

   Laban

   Leah

   Rachel

2. Naomi talks about how Leah longed to be loved by her husband Jacob. How is a woman affected when she longs for love from someone very close to her but feels consistent rejection instead?

3. **Read:** Genesis 29:31–35. One critically important moment in Leah's life was when she realized that the Lord *saw her!* How did God see Leah and what did he do for her?

4. What do you learn about how Leah saw her life in the naming of her first three sons? How does Leah's outlook on life begin to change with the birth of her fourth son?

5. Leah finally discovered that her meaning and value were not in her husband or even in her children, but in her relationship to the Lord. Why was this so important for Leah and why is it so necessary in our own lives and journeys of faith? In what way is this a struggle for you?

6. Naomi tells about the first time she really felt the deep love of God. She called her sister and said, "He sees me and he loves me!" If you can, share a time when you experienced the deep and abiding love of God in a very personal way. How does God's love for you shape how you see yourself?

> *"Leah never gained the affection she longed for from her husband, but she was not poor! She found favor and affection in the eyes of her heavenly Father."*
>
> **Naomi Zacharias**

7. **Read:** Genesis 30:1–24. Somewhere along the way, Rachael and Leah began a jealous, competitive battle to see who could produce the most children. How do you respond to this part of their story? In what way can you personally relate to it?

8. How has the affection and love of God carried you through those times when you did not receive or feel loved by the people around you?

"If Leah judged herself and her success by her husband Jacob, she would have been sad all of the time, but if she measured herself by the way God saw her, joy would be hers."

Naomi Zacharias

9. Naomi presents three "gems of learning" we receive when we allow ourselves to really hear Leah's story: (1) life is not flawless and can be hard; (2) we must sometimes live with unanswered questions and unfulfilled longings; (3) no matter how invisible we might feel in this life, we are always seen by God himself. How can these lessons help women as they walk through life and face real pain and rejection?

Which one of these gems speaks into a situation in your life at this time? Explain.

10. It may surprise you to learn that Jesus came through the bloodline of Jacob and Leah and not through Jacob and Rachel. What encouragement does this give to you as we live in a culture that lifts up the "beautiful people" and tends to ignore those who seem "ordinary"?

"We cannot transform society's opinion of beauty, but what we can change each day is our perception of beauty, our recognition of it in its right place, that it is lovely and something to be admired, but a deeper recognition that it is not where the true life legacy of an individual lies."

Naomi Zacharias

Group Prayer Direction

- Ask God to help you see yourself as he does, beautiful and valuable.
- Pray that you will not be captured by the lies of the world about what true beauty is.
- Pray for daughters, granddaughters, nieces, and other girls, asking God to protect them from the damage and pain of basing their value on looks or what people say about them.
- Thank God for how he uses all kinds of people, including the "Leahs" of this world.
- Pray that the women in your group will hear God say, "I see you and I love you." And ask for this message to be so clear that each of you lives with the daily awareness that you are precious and loved more than you dream!

Journal Between Sessions

How has the pressure in our world to "look beautiful" affected your heart and influenced your faith journey?

_____

_____

_____

_____

_____

_____

_____

_____

_____

_____

_____

_____

_____

_____

_____

_____

_____

_____

HANNAH

SURRENDERING IN WAITING

Key Scripture:
1 Samuel 1:1–20

Amena Brown

MEETING HANNAH

Hannah was a woman of deep faith, passionate devotion, and amazing patience. She lived over three thousand years ago in a world very different than ours, but she faced many of the same challenges and struggles women face today.

Hannah was the wife of a man named Elkanah, who was also married to a woman named Peninnah. This may seem strange to women in our modern world, but it was common for men in the ancient world to have more than one wife.

We learn that Elkanah's wife Peninnah "had children, but Hannah had none." Childlessness was one of the worst hardships a woman in that culture could endure. On top of the natural pain of longing to have children but not being able to conceive, Hannah had an additional pain to bear—the constant taunting and provoking that came from her rival, Peninnah.

But Hannah refused to retaliate or seek revenge. Instead, she wept and prayed to the Lord. She was honest about her struggle and submissive to God's plan for her life. She poured her heart out to the Lord . . . and then she waited. At last the Lord heard her cry and answered her prayer for a son.

When a son was born to Elkanah and Hannah, they named him Samuel, which means "heard of God." One of the most shocking and amazing things we learn about Hannah is that after seeing her dreams fulfilled, she offered her son back to God. Just as she had promised, Hannah brought young Samuel to the tabernacle and handed him over to the priest, Eli, so that Samuel could serve the Lord all the days of his life. Hannah's little boy grew into a mighty man of God, a Spirit-led prophet, and leader of God's people.

Hannah's life bears witness that God listens to our cries and that he does, indeed, answer prayers. Hannah modeled patience and a willingness to wait on God and trust him, even when things looked hopeless. She was a real woman who faced real heartache, real conflict, and yet chose to exercise her faith in a way that stands as an example for all of us today.

Introduction

Have you ever been to an amusement park? Have you spent a whole day with family or friends at Disneyland, Disney World, Six Flags, or the like? If you have, you know what it feels like to stand in a line and wait. These "fun" experiences can feel like a day of waiting punctuated by two-minute rides that bring joy and delight.

Often, our lives feel like a day at the amusement park. We spend a good portion of our lives waiting. Certainly, there are the mundane moments that fill each day, times when we stand in line at a store or get stuck at every red light on the way to church. But there are also the longer waiting experiences, the times when our dreams and hopes go unfulfilled for weeks, months, even years. We wait for our schedule to finally slow down so we can get time for ourselves. We wait to find love, to have children, for a new career direction, for that promotion we've deserved, for our retirement, and for countless other things. The truth is that much of life is spent waiting for something!

What if we saw these times of waiting as opportunities to embrace rather than obstacles to overcome. Wise women learn to leverage the moments and seasons of waiting as a chance to grow deeper in their faith. Contrary to what we often think, waiting can be a gift from God, an experience that shapes us into the women he wants us to be.

In this session, we are invited to see ourselves in the story of Hannah. God was present with Hannah as she waited, and he is with us as well in those moments in our lives when patience is needed and endurance is required. Perhaps those moments of delay—and even the longer seasons of waiting—are more than minor irritations or major frustrations. These experiences just might be opportunities for God to transform us and teach us to truly value what matters most—his loving ability to meet all of our needs.

Talk About It

Briefly respond as a group to one of the following questions.

Share a childhood memory about waiting for something. How did you feel when you finally got what you were waiting for?

Tell about a time you were in a season of waiting for something (or someone) and how this process strengthened, refined, or grew you in some way.

"We should live our lives in a fluid dance of surrender with God. You have to surrender, and surrender often."

Amena Brown

Video Teaching Notes

Hannah's story

What to do when we are forced to wait

God's greater story

We are always waiting for something

We are always waiting to get "there"

Lessons from Hannah's journey

God sees you

Expect irritation

Pour out your emotions to the Lord

Surrender

> *"God does not want your happy face if you are not happy. He wants your real face!"*
>
> *Amena Brown*

Small Group Study and Video Discussion

1. **Read:** 1 Samuel 1:1–20. In this passage we read that "the LORD" had closed Hannah's womb. What effect does this act of God have on Hannah's life?

   How do you respond to the idea that God might actually use something hard and deeply painful to grow us and write a deeper story in our lives?

2. First Samuel 1:6 says that Peninnah kept provoking Hannah to irritate her because she could not have children. What can we learn from Hannah's response as we encounter the "Peninnahs" in our own lives?

3. Hannah cried out to God from a sincere, devoted, and passionate heart, totally honest with him about her desire and longing for a child. Share a time when you cried out to God on a deep level and he answered your prayer with a "yes!"

What is something that you have prayed for but have not yet received a "yes" from God?

4. Sometimes we receive what we long for, only to find that it isn't all we had wanted. Describe a time when you waited for something and once it arrived it led you into another season of waiting.

"'Here' is never good enough; 'there' just seems like it is going to be so much better."

Amena Brown

5. We can often spend our time and energy focusing on "there" and miss what God is doing "here." What helps you focus more fully on the "here and now" and keeps you from living too much in the "then and there"?

How can you deepen your ability to recognize and respond to God's presence day by day, moment by moment?

> *"Maybe it is time to learn that there is a lot more to being 'here' than you think!"*
>
> **Amena Brown**

6. Hannah brought her honest emotions to God. And God heard her cries. Hannah reminds us that God does not expect us to "hold it together" and "be strong" all the time. Why do you think we often try to act like we have it all together?

   How might our relationship with God and others change if we tried our best to be honest?

7. Amena points out, "Whatever you are waiting for, it seems like everyone else is getting that very thing!" What can we do to respond in a godly manner when everyone else seems to be getting the very thing we long for?

8. When Hannah finally had Samuel and held him in her arms, she made a choice to give him back to God. Talk about a time when you knew you were called to give something or someone up to God, but you were resistant or afraid. How did you respond in that situation? If you chose to surrender that something or someone, what happened as a result?

9. What in your life right now do you need to give to God, and how can your group members pray for you and encourage you as you seek to live with open hands and a surrendered heart?

"I prayed for this child, and the LORD has granted me what I asked of him. So now I give him to the LORD. For his whole life he will be given over to the LORD."

1 Samuel 1:27–28

Group Prayer Direction

- Thank God for his faithfulness and the prayers he has answered in the past and let him know that you want to trust him for the future.
- Pray for contentment in your "here."
- Pray for people you love and care about who are struggling with infertility and are crying out to God as they wait on him.
- Ask God to help you surrender those times of waiting in your life as you come honestly to him.
- Thank God for being with you in your times of waiting, even when he has felt far away.

Journal Between Sessions

Pour your heart out to God honestly about some of life's situations that presently have you in a waiting pattern.

_____

_____

_____

_____

_____

_____

_____

_____

_____

_____

_____

_____

_____

_____

_____

_____

_____

_____

_____

_____

ABIGAIL

DEALING WITH CONFRONTATION IN RELATIONSHIPS

Key Scripture:
1 Samuel 25:1–39

Elisa Morgan

MEETING ABIGAIL

We are told Abigail was a beautiful woman. We assume this passage is describing her outward beauty, but it does not take long for us to see that this accurately reflects her inner self as well. Abigail was a woman of wisdom and discernment. She had a sharp mind and a generous spirit. And, as we see in her interaction with David, she was also a woman of peace.

Abigail stands out as a person of character and consistency in a time when these traits were in short supply. She possessed strength and resolve, qualities that led her to take risks, step into the fray, and willingly sacrifice for the sake of others.

Without a doubt, Abigail was a woman of godly character, and yet we soon learn that she is the mirror opposite of her husband. His name, Nabal, gives us the clearest sense of his character: it literally means "fool"! He was surly, impulsive, and flat-out mean. He lacked the self-control, wisdom, and discernment possessed by his wife.

When conflict arose between Nabal and David, Abigail did not run from the situation. In fact, she used many of her gifts to calm the chaos. Abigail acted to protect two men who had grown hotheaded and argumentative. She refused to sit by passively and simply let the conflict escalate. Instead, she chose to confront it.

Her actions are even more remarkable when we remember that Abigail lived in a time and place when women were often ostracized and marginalized. Ancient leaders did not typically bring women into their confidence or listen to their advice. But Abigail's advice was heard and respected. With sensitivity and strength she spoke into a conflicted relationship. And so she still stands as a model peacemaker—a woman who stood up with boldness and diffused relational landmines with wisdom and tact.

Introduction

No one really enjoys conflict. If possible, most of us prefer to avoid confrontations. The world around us is filled with tension, with constant news of war and political unrest, and all we want is a little peace and quiet. When relationships feel strained, our knee-jerk reaction is to look the other way, bury our head in the sand, and hope it all goes away.

The problem is that relational tensions rarely go away by simply ignoring them. Conflicts tend to fester and grow worse. When they eventually surface, the results can be disastrous.

All through the Bible we learn that confronting painful and conflicted situations is exactly what God wants us to do. Jesus addressed this with crystal-clear teaching: "If your brother or sister sins, go and point out their fault, just between the two of you. If they listen to you, you have won them over. But if they will not listen, take one or two others along, so that 'every matter may be established by the testimony of two or three witnesses'" (Matthew 18:15–16). Jesus was clear that relationships were of the utmost importance to him, and they should be important to us as well (Matthew 22:39). Jesus went so far as to say that we have permission to walk out of church in the middle of a worship service if the goal is to heal a broken relationship (Matthew 5:23–25).

In this session we meet a woman who understood the value of gentle, but honest confrontation. Abigail did not shy away from seeking healing in relationships, even when it meant confronting others. In a time and culture when women were often marginalized, Abigail stands out as a shining example of love in action. Her example reminds us that relationships are valuable and we must do whatever we can to keep them healthy and whole, even if we must deal with tough issues and have those difficult conversations we'd rather not have.

Talk About It

Briefly respond as a group to one of the following questions.

How do you respond when you need to have a difficult conversation with someone you love? And conversely, how do you respond when you are confronted by others?

Describe a time when someone had a "hard-to-have" conversation with you, or a time you initiated a "hard-to-have" conversation with someone else. How did it turn out?

"Those of us who know God, who are called into a relationship with him, who want to live our lives according to his Word, are called to find our voice and to have those hard-to-have conversations in such a way to resolve conflicts in a healthy manner."

Elisa Morgan

Video Teaching Notes

Finding your voice in difficult situations: learning from Abigail

The main characters in the story

Three conflicts in the story:

#1–Employer and employee

#2–Husband and wife

#3–God versus his people, specifically God and anointed David

Abigail finds her voice:

She cogitates

She participates

She negotiates

She advocates

> "You belong to God and you are one of God's children. You are connected to God."
>
> *Elisa Morgan*

Small Group Study and Video Discussion

1. **Read:** 1 Samuel 25:2–13. How would you describe the contrast between Abigail and her husband Nabal?

2. **Read:** 1 Samuel 25:14–17. When we face a situation that is conflict laden, why is it critical that we take time to cogitate and think very deeply and seriously?

What are some possible results if we fail to cogitate?

3. **Read:** 1 Samuel 25:18–39. Abigail kept encouraging the right behavior even though Nabal and David were not acting in godly ways. How did Abigail show wisdom and humility as she negotiated and related with both of these men?

4. What are some practical ways we can negotiate and become a peacemaker in conflict-filled situations?

5. What is one conflicted situation you are facing in this season of your life?

What negotiating skills might help you make it through this time of conflict?

6. Abigail not only advocates for David, but she boldly advocates for herself. She asks David to remember her after the conflict is resolved. She dares, in the middle of the furnace of conflict, to speak for herself and her future. Why do you think some women are hesitant to advocate for themselves?

"Remember whose you are and who you are!"

Elisa Morgan

7. Tell about a situation in your life where you need to respond with one or more of the four principles Elisa shared:

Cogitate

Participate

Negotiate

Advocate

How can your small group pray for you as you seek to take action in this relationship in one of these specific areas?

"To all who did receive him, to those who believed in his name, he gave the right to become children of God."

John 1:12

Group Prayer Direction

- Ask God to give you and the other women in your group discernment and wisdom for those hard-to-have conversations.
- Pray for the women in your group who are in tough and conflicted situations.
- Praise God for calling us to be peacemakers in our homes, workplaces, and everywhere he leads us.
- Pray that our character will be strengthened as we interact with the people in authority over us.
- Pray for the women who are married. Ask God to strengthen their marriage and pray for wisdom to know when to confront and how to do it in a redemptive way.

Journal Between Sessions

What characteristics of Abigail do you want to see grow in your life? Journal about specific situations where these characteristics in you would be pleasing to God and ask him to guide and strengthen you to live in these new ways.

_____

_____

_____

_____

_____

_____

_____

_____

_____

_____

_____

_____

_____

_____

_____

_____

GOMER

LEARNING TO ACCEPT UNCONDITIONAL LOVE

Key Scriptures: Hosea 1:2–11 and 2:14–3:5

Jeanne Stevens

MEETING GOMER

She was a prostitute who became the wife of the local prophet. Can you imagine the whispers and conversations that would have taken place around the dinner tables, in hair salons, and at the grocery store if the local pastor married the local hooker?

The story of Gomer does not have a "happily ever after" ending. Gomer had three children while married and living with her husband Hosea, but because she continued to sleep around with other men, no one really knew who had fathered the children. After the birth of her third child, Gomer grew tired of her marriage and ran off to live with another man . . . and then another, until eventually she ended up back on the streets.

Gomer left her husband and abandoned her children. Why? To return to a life of prostitution. The local prophet's wife could be bought for a small price and any man in town could have his way with her. Gomer was certainly not an example we would be encouraged to model our lives after. And yet, her story speaks a powerful word of grace and acceptance to us today.

What happens next is almost unbelievable. While Gomer is wallowing in the depth of her rebellion and sin, God calls her abandoned husband, Hosea, to keep on loving her anyway. God tells Hosea that he is to open his heart and home once again to the woman who has rejected him and scorned his embrace. With great humility, Hosea walks up to the leader of the prostitution ring and buys back his own wife.

What a heartrending, yet beautiful picture of gracious love. Hosea's love for his unfaithful wife models God's unconditional love for sinful people. This is a love that faces betrayal, unfaithfulness, deceit, and abandonment with forgiveness and mercy.

Introduction

The story of Gomer and Hosea is a picture of God's unconditional love for his children. God called Hosea to marry Gomer and love her through all of her wanderings and unfaithfulness because Hosea was going to bring a message to the people of Israel—a message about the faithful love of their heavenly Father. There are three distinct levels for us to relate to in this story.

At the most basic level this is a story about a real man and a real woman. Hosea and Gomer's story is a tragedy filled with deceit and brokenness. It is also a reminder that it is possible to forgive those who have hurt us, even when a relationship seems to have been shattered beyond repair.

Second, this is a story about God and his people. Just like Gomer, the nation of Israel had wandered from the one who had loved them and called them his own. God's people are prone to wander from wholehearted devotion to the Lord and easily forget that only God deserves their love. Idols cry out for our attention, and when we look to something or someone other than God for our deliverance, it breaks the heart of our Father. But God doesn't abandon us, even though we have rejected him. He keeps loving us, seeking us, and inviting us back into a relationship with him. He loves us so much that he allowed his precious and only Son to die for our sins. That is unconditional love!

Third, the story of Gomer is our story as individuals. God loves women like you and me. Even when we wander, find other sources of comfort, or neglect to spend time with him . . . his love never fails. He opens his arms and invites us to come back home again.

As you watch Gomer's drama unfold you may be shocked at her hardheartedness and her rebellion. You may be taken aback by her treatment of her husband and her three children. But remember that Gomer is simply a mirror to our own lives. Her life and her actions are meant to help us see our own failures and discover that we are really no different. We, too, have wandered, rebelled, and been unfaithful to God. Gomer reminds us of our own failures, but her story is also a reflection of God's grace, patience, and never-ending love for us.

> *"God never stops loving us. He never stops pursuing us. He never stops wanting a relationship with us. . . . This is good news."*
>
> **Jeanne Stevens**

Talk About It

Briefly respond as a group to one of the following questions.

If you have a family history or some special meaning behind your name, share it with the group.

What Bible story surprises or shocks you and makes you wonder, "Why did God put this in his Holy Word?"

> *"We usually look at the offenses of others before we look at our own; we look at their problems before we look at our own flaws. It is much easier to look at someone else's mess-ups and little blemishes instead of looking into the mirror."*
>
> **Jeanne Stevens**

Video Teaching Notes

The story of Hosea and Gomer

Good news, bad news

Hosea's and Gomer's three children and the meaning of their names (symbols of Israel's relationship with God)

A son, Jezreel: "God scatters"

A daughter, Lo-Ruhamah: "no mercy"

A son, Lo-Ammi: "not mine, nobody"

Broken promises

Covering up and comparing

Hidden flaws

Naming a child

God's unconditional love

Small Group Study and Video Discussion

1. **Read:** Hosea 1:2–11. Hosea was the local prophet, the equivalent of today's town pastor. How do you think he felt and what might have gone through his mind when God called him to marry Gomer?

   Why do you think this picture of adultery is the one God chose in order to show us a picture of ourselves with him?

2. How do the names of Gomer's children—Jezreel ("God will scatter"), Lo-Ruhamah ("no mercy"), and Lo-Ammi ("not my people")—serve as warnings to the people of Israel?

   How do God's words of Hosea 1:10–11 offer promise and hope despite these prophetic warnings?

3. **Read:** Hosea 2:14–17. What are some of the specific ways God says he will use to win back the heart of his people? How will his people respond to his love?

4. **Read:** Hosea 3:1–5. Gomer has abandoned Hosea, the local pastor/prophet, and she is now selling herself as a prostitute. Yet God calls Hosea to buy her out of slavery and love her again. If you were Hosea, how would you have responded to this? What do you think it would have felt like to be Gomer in this situation?

5. **Read:** Matthew 7:2–4. Jeanne says that our natural human tendency is to notice the sins of others before we notice our own. How do you see this in your life?

What is the danger of this pattern?

"As women we can become champions at covering up and comparing."

Jeanne Stevens

6. Following are some of the poignant lessons we learn when we look at Gomer. What is *one* lesson that hits home for you and what is God speaking to your heart through Gomer's story?

- We are hopeless outside of God.
- We can betray who God created us to be.
- We can sabotage ourselves and others.
- We can neglect God.
- We can resist the way God wants us to live.
- We try to take control of our life instead of trusting God.
- We do what we need to make sure our desires are met instead of waiting on God to meet our needs.

"Sometimes we subtly, or even overtly, betray who God designed us to be."

Jeanne Stevens

7. What connections do you see between: Gomer's unfaithfulness to Hosea, Israel's fickle love for God, and our tendency to wander from God and forget the depth of his love for us?

"No matter where your story has taken you, you can always come back home. Only God can heal your pain."

Jeanne Stevens

8. **Read:** Hosea 2:23. Later in the story, God promises a reversal of the harsh judgment he had earlier spoken about. The illicit children of Gomer are given more positive and optimistic names and welcomed into the family. What are Gomer's children renamed and what is the significance of this transformation?

What does this say to us about God's relationship and how he wants to treat us, even with our sin and brokenness?

9. What are some of the things in our lives that can become a "first love" and take God's place? What can we do to identify and avoid these enticements and make sure our heart is fully devoted to God?

"I will plant her for myself in the land; I will show my love to the one I called 'Not my loved one.' I will say to those called 'Not my people,' 'You are my people'; and they will say, 'You are my God.'"

Hosea 2:23

Group Prayer Direction

◎ Thank God for his unending love and faithfulness, even when we go astray; that he is always willing to welcome us back home, no matter where our story may have taken us.

◎ Pray for courage and humility to look honestly at places where you may be covering up or comparing.

◎ Ask God to give you a greater hunger for him.

◎ Pray for people you love who have wandered far from God and need to hear his invitation to come back home.

Journal Between Sessions

Jeanne tells the story about her desire for her kids to look good in front of others. Are there areas or experiences in your life that you find yourself covering up and trying to look good? Journal about these areas and seek God for freedom in these areas.

_____

_____

_____

_____

_____

_____

_____

_____

_____

_____

_____

_____

_____

_____

_____

_____

_____

_____

_____

_____

MARY, MOTHER OF JESUS

MOVING FROM COMFORT TO COURAGE

Key Scripture:
Luke 1:26–38

Jeanne Stevens

MEETING MARY

*W*hen we first encounter Mary in the story of Scripture she is a teenage girl betrothed to a man named Joseph. Mary was a real person, with a real family, real friends, a real faith in God, and the very real feelings of an ordinary teenage girl.

So when the angel Gabriel appeared to her one day and announced that the Lord was with her, Mary likely had no idea what was coming next! Gabriel then explained that she would become pregnant and give birth to the one who would be "the Son of the Most High." Without a doubt, this young virgin would have experienced a mix of fear and amazement, just like any ordinary girl.

But Mary's response to the angel gives us a window into the heart of this woman of faith. Despite her youth, Mary willingly surrendered her life, her future, and her own dreams to God when she said, "I am the Lord's servant," and "May it be as you have said." Don't miss the importance of these statements. This courageous willingness to follow God—whatever he would ask of her—marked the life of Mary from the very beginning.

Undoubtedly, she had to suffer through the stares, whispers, and gossip of those who didn't buy the whole angel-and-virgin-birth explanation for her condition. But, in her heart, Mary believed God and she went on to bear and deliver the promised child.

Mary raised her son, Jesus, and watched him mature from a child to a young man. Eventually, her beloved boy went from being her son to her Savior. And Mary was there at the end of his life, just as she had been there at the beginning. She walked with Jesus to the cross, as any loving mother would have done. Though the life story of Mary is missing many of the specific details we would like to know, one thing is clear and certain: Mary was chosen of God and her faithfulness, courage, and devotion are a beautiful model of a heart submitted to the Lord and his will for our lives.

Introduction

If someone ever tries to tell you that following God is easy, be careful! There is a good chance they are trying to sell you something. The Scriptures are quite clear that the opposite is true—following God is impossible in our own strength. It is only possible for those who learn to lean upon God in faith and trusting obedience.

Jesus himself taught his disciples that following him would be like carrying a cross, a journey of pain, sacrifice, and self-denial: "Whoever wants to be my disciple must deny themselves and take up their cross daily and follow me" (Luke 9:23). The apostle Paul wrote, "Everyone who wants to live a godly life in Christ Jesus will be persecuted" (2 Timothy 3:12). And Peter warned us not to be surprised at the difficulty of following God: "Do not be surprised at the fiery ordeal that has come on you to test you, as though something strange were happening to you" (1 Peter 4:12). In fact, James even encouraged us to remember that God uses our trials to mature us in faith. They are a hidden blessing from his hand, and a reason to rejoice: "Consider it pure joy . . . whenever you face trials of many kinds" (James 1:2).

Following Jesus and submitting to God's leading is an invitation to transition from comfort to courage. God never promises that walking with him will be a painless and easy path. Instead, he assures us of his presence: that he will be near us and never leave us. When we follow the leading of God's Holy Spirit, life becomes an adventure, demanding a level of courage that will stretch each of us to the breaking point.

In this session we meet Mary, a woman of extraordinary and consistent courage. As we observe her journey of faith, we will find ourselves longing for the courage we need to take risks, follow God with greater passion, and submit to the Lord's will more quickly and confidently.

If you are looking for advice on how to grow more comfortable or want an easy shortcut to maturity in faith, you won't find that in the story of Mary. But if you are ready to be challenged and to face situations that will demand fresh courage and stretch your limits, Mary's life is a case study you will want to read and study over and over again!

Talk About It

Briefly respond as a group to one of the following questions.

When we think of courage and a daring spirit, we often think of doing risky or extreme things. Tell about a time you took a risk, tried something a little daring, or really went out on a limb and did something that demanded courage.

Name one woman you know, or know about, who you would say is courageous. What makes this woman courageous in your mind?

"Mary's real faith is a picture of unbelievable courage. To trust God was to be courageous."

Jeanne Stevens

Video Teaching Notes

Mary, an ordinary Jewish teenager called to an extraordinary task

Mary, a woman of courage

Mary's courageous decision: "May it be!"

Stories of "may it be" kinds of courage

Mary, an example to all women to be courageous

Moving from comfort to courage

We are invited to a "may it be" kind of faith

> *"'May it be!' These just might be the most courageous words Mary uttered throughout her whole life!"*
>
> **Jeanne Stevens**

Small Group Study and Video Discussion

1. **Read:** Luke 1:26–38. What do you learn about Mary through her interaction with the angel Gabriel?

   In verse 38, Mary responds with a level of agreement and acceptance that is shocking. What does this one simple line reveal about her heart and her relationship to God?

2. Tell about a time you told God "may it be" and yielded a new part of your heart, future, or life to God's will.

How has your life changed since that time of surrender?

3. Jeanne wrote in her personal journal that she believes courage will always require an element of leaving. Have you found this to be true in your own life and why do you think this is the case?

"Courage always demands an element of leaving, and leaving is always hard!"

Jeanne Stevens

4. Jeanne notes some things that can happen when we live with "may it be" courage as Mary did. From the following list, choose one or two areas in which you might need to take a step of courage.

- Have the ability to act regardless of the feelings, consequences, or circumstances
- Trust God even when I don't have the answers
- Say I am sorry when I know I am at fault
- Admit "I don't know" when I realize I don't know
- Say "I love you" despite the hurt, anger, or fear I feel
- Some other area I need courage _____

What is keeping you from taking this step and how can your group members cheer you on as you take the next step to follow God with renewed courage?

> *"Moving from comfort to courage will cause you to question your decision. It will cause you to look around for the safety bars, seatbelt, and any kind of security button."*
>
> **Jeanne Stevens**

5. Jeanne says, "Moving from comfort to courage will cause you to pray like never before." How has your prayer life grown when you have taken risks to follow and live for God with a courageous heart?

> *"Moving from comfort to courage will cause you to feel weak in the knees—a good indicator that you should stop standing up and get ON your knees."*
>
> **Jeanne Stevens**

6. We all have areas in our lives where God is prompting us to make a move from comfort to courage, yet we resist and drag our feet. In these moments, prayer can be just what we need to get the process started. How can your group members pray for you in one specific area of your life where you know God wants you to take a courageous step forward?

How do you need to begin praying for yourself in this area?

"Just like God invaded the life of Mary and called her into a courageous faith, God is inviting his daughters today into that same kind of life of 'may it be' courage."

Jeanne Stevens

Group Prayer Direction

- Pray that you and your group members will exhibit Mary's "may it be" kind of faith.
- Thank God that when you move from comfort to courage he always shows up and leads you through whatever you face.
- Pray that you and your group members will be honest (with self, others, and God) when tempted to cover up.
- Celebrate and give thanks to God for the areas of your lives in which you have followed God's call to move from comfort to courage.
- Pray for those you love and care about who have not yet accepted the life-changing love and grace of Jesus. Ask God to help them see the depth of his sacrificial love for them.

Journal Between Sessions

Think about the areas of your life where God has been calling you to a "may it be" kind of faith walk. Journal honestly about the fears, struggles, concerns, and cautions you have when you think about surrendering these areas to him.

_____

_____

_____

_____

_____

_____

_____

_____

_____

_____

_____

_____

_____

_____

_____

_____

_____

_____

_____

_____

MARY MAGDALENE

TRANSFORMING FROM OUTCAST TO FOLLOWER

Key Scriptures: Luke 8:1–2; John 19:25; and 20:1–18

Jonalyn Fincher

MEETING MARY MAGDALENE

*M*ary Magdalene was a woman filled with zeal, passion, and fervor! If we could look inside her and see her heart, we would find a woman who had experienced deep pain and brokenness, a woman who bore the scars of her past. We know that she had been delivered of seven demons, evil powers that had taken over her life. Jesus cast these demons out of her, setting her free.

Take a moment to stop and really think about the life of this woman. She had seven demonic beings attacking, tormenting, and directing her life. It is hard for us to really grasp the emotional, psychological, relational, and spiritual damage this left in her life. This was someone who knew deep pain.

But if we could look into Mary's heart, we would also see a depth of love and longing for Jesus that would inspire each of us to thirst for more of the Savior. It was Jesus who had cured her and set her free. And Mary Magdalene knew the Savior's power in a very personal way. She had been a direct recipient of God's extravagant power, grace, and love in Jesus.

She was also honored by God to be the first witness to encounter the resurrected Jesus. In a time and culture when women were not even trusted to bear witness in a court, Jesus called Mary to be the first witness to his resurrection. Jesus trusted her to share what she had seen and heard from him with others.

Mary's life is a story of radical extremes. Bound by demons, she was freed by Jesus. A woman with no social standing, Mary became an honored witness to the resurrection. From outcast to included follower of Jesus, Mary traveled an amazing journey to sit at the feet of Jesus. Her life is a reminder to each of us that no matter where we are or where we have been, we are never beyond the powerful touch of Jesus. Jesus still sets women free from the demons that torment them and control their lives. He still invites women to follow him. And he still calls us to be his witnesses to the world.

Introduction

Everyone whose life has been touched by Jesus has a testimony to share. We all have a story of the transformation that God has brought to our life. Mary Magdalene's story certainly wasn't boring! She had been delivered from demonic oppression to follow Jesus . . . all the way to his tragic death on the cross. But Mary's testimony doesn't end there. She was the first witness to the most significant event in all of human history—the resurrection of God's Son!

Her life is a story of transformation, and it's worth examining in more detail.

In this session we will look at the journey of Mary Magdalene and we'll learn that each of us has a story to tell. Our story may not be like Mary's, but regardless of our past, our pain, our struggles, or our demons, Jesus has a plan for our future that is more glorious than we could possibly dream.

We have been set free and are being set free.

We have been delivered and are being delivered.

We are trusted by God, and entrusted with the good news of Jesus.

We are witnesses that Jesus is alive and we have been invited to share this amazing truth with the world.

Talk About It

Briefly respond as a group to one of the following questions.

Our culture seems to have ways of declaring people either "in" or "out." What places a person in the inner circle and what makes a person an outcast?

Tell about a time you ended up on the outside and felt like an outcast.

> "God created humans to be his image, to be reflections of him on earth, men and women to reflect God's nature."
>
> **Jonalyn Fincher**

Video Teaching Notes

A woman growing up in the first-century culture

The status of women in the ancient world

Mary of Bethany's example

Jesus delivers Mary Magdalene and gives her a hope-filled future

Mary's journey with Jesus

The resurrected Jesus appears to Mary

Jesus says Mary's name and gives her instructions

We are reflections of God's nature

Metaphor of broken shards

The scarred Savior works in the scarred places of our lives

"Jesus takes the broken shards of our lives and mends them back together so we can reflect Jesus."

Jonalyn Fincher

Small Group Study and Video Discussion

1. **Read:** Luke 8:1–2; John 19:25; and 20:1–18. Jonalyn gives some historical background on the role and place of women in first-century Palestine. How might growing up in such a culture shape the way a young woman might have seen herself?

2. When Mary first met Jesus, he delivered her from demonic beings that were controlling her life. As you look back on your own life, from what controlling powers has Jesus delivered you? How have you experienced freedom as a follower of Christ?

"Do not fear, for I have redeemed you; I have summoned you by name; you are mine."

Isaiah 43:1

3. Jonalyn says that Mary of Bethany may have given Mary Magdalene a picture of one who takes the time to sit at the feet of Jesus. After his resurrection, the Scriptures tell us that Mary Magdalene also knelt at the feet of Jesus, her beloved teacher. What are some ways in which you seek to kneel at the feet of Jesus as a worshipper and student?

"Choose Jesus and he will not be taken away from you."

Jonalyn Fincher

4. What can we do to spend more time at the feet of Jesus? What gets in the way of us doing this?

5. Jesus entrusted Mary Magdalene to be the first person to bear a message to the disciples after his resurrection. She must have been overwhelmed and amazed that God would give her such a calling. What is something God has entrusted to you that amazes and surprises you? How are you seeking to fulfill this calling?

"Like Mary Magdalene, in our brokenness we feel the most ashamed; it seems to me the places I have been most broken, I am most reluctant to hand over to Jesus."

Jonalyn Fincher

6. Jonalyn notes how the places we have experienced the greatest measure of brokenness can be the areas of our lives we are most reluctant to hand over to Jesus. What is an area of your life you have not fully yielded to God and how can your group members pray for you and keep you accountable to continue surrendering this part of your life to the Savior?

"Of all the religions in the world, Christianity is the only one where our Savior and God bears scars in his body."

Jonalyn Fincher

Group Prayer Direction

- Pray that God would mend the broken places in our lives.
- Pray for deliverance from the evil influences in our lives.
- Ask God to help you and the members of your group see yourselves the way he does.
- Pray that you will become bold because Jesus is in you.
- Pray that you would grow in your understanding of the sweetness of worshipping at the feet of Jesus. Ask God to help each of you long for time to sit at the feet of the Savior.
- Thank God that he has shown us his love so powerfully through Jesus.
- Pray that you will be a faithful witness of the love and message of Jesus.

Journal Between Sessions

Jonalyn talks about how Mary must have felt broken and ashamed because of her past. Hers was a journey of experiencing the healing touch of Jesus putting together the broken pieces of her life. Journal about how Jesus has brought healing to your life and how is he putting together your broken pieces. Thank him for past healing and ask him to continue his work of restoration.

MARY OF BETHANY

PUTTING OUR FAITH INTO ACTION

Key Scripture:
Mark 14:1–9

Elisa Morgan

MEETING MARY OF BETHANY

*M*ary of Bethany was known for many things. For one, she had a sister named Martha who was a diligent worker, famous for her hospitality. There is even a story in the Scriptures about a time when Mary was reprimanded by Martha for sitting at the feet of Jesus instead of helping with the work.

Mary's brother, Lazarus, was famous for another reason: Jesus had raised him from the dead! I'm sure people may have pointed Mary out on the street as the sister of her famous brother: "You see that woman, her name is Mary, she's the sister of Lazarus!"

But Mary was more than just the sister of Martha and Lazarus. Mary was the one who sat at the feet of Jesus whenever he was around, longing to be in his presence and drinking in his teaching. In a world where women were often marginalized and kept from receiving religious training, Mary was a student, hungry to learn and receive the words of Jesus.

Jesus often visited the home of Mary, Martha, and Lazarus when he traveled through Bethany. He was a friend of the family. But over time Jesus became more than a friend. Mary came to know and believe that Jesus was more than a gifted rabbi—he was the long-awaited Messiah! In a profound act of worship, Mary took one of her most valuable and costly possessions, a jar of pure nard, and poured it over the head of Jesus. In fact, this act of worship was so profound that Jesus himself linked Mary's sacrificial gift with the telling of the gospel. Jesus told his followers that for all time and in all places, whenever the gospel is shared, the story of Mary would be told as well.

Mary never took Jesus for granted. Whenever she had time and opportunity to be in his presence she made listening to him a top priority. Mary loved Jesus, and she was commended by Jesus for the quality of her love—wholehearted and devoted.

Introduction

"What can one person do?" Maybe you've asked yourself that very question. Overwhelmed by the needs of the world or seemingly insurmountable obstacles, we can easily start to wonder if our efforts to love and serve people in Jesus' name really make much of a difference. Questions lead to doubts, doubt leads to despair, and soon we are paralyzed by the size of the task before us, unable to move forward.

Mary of Bethany was an ordinary woman, just like you. She lived in a world filled with problems and needs. But as we hear her story, we discover that she was not content to simply sit back. Mary was a woman of action. Her attitude was simple and pure: "I will do what I can!" Her default response to the needs of others was a question: "What can I do or contribute?"

Mary was honored by Jesus for her initiative and her extravagant devotion. After anointing his head with expensive perfume, several of those present were critical of Mary for "wasting" her resources on Jesus. They argued that her meager resources could have been put to a more appropriate use, perhaps to help the poor or feed the hungry. But Jesus rebuked them and blessed Mary for her devotion and love. In the words of Jesus, Mary "did what she could." And she did it for him.

Mary reminds us that we aren't called to solve the world's problems—poverty, hunger, injustice—on our own, but we *can* do something. And if we serve out of love and devotion to Jesus, our meager efforts will be rewarded and remembered by the One who *does* have the power to change the world.

> "Mary of Bethany understood who Jesus was, she somehow got that he was the Messiah, that he was going to the cross for the sins of all humankind and for her. And in this moment she did what alone she could do. She gave to Jesus what she could give."
>
> *Elisa Morgan*

Talk About It

Briefly respond as a group to one of the following questions.

Which needs that are facing our world make you say, "I wish I could do something to help"?

Tell about a time you took a small step and entered into our hurting world, and how God worked through that commitment.

Video Teaching Notes

We live with needs all around us

Mark 14:8: "She did what she could"

She *did* what she could

She did *what* she could

She did what she *could*

What if I did what I could?

Mary of Bethany wanted to love Jesus back

By doing what we can, we love Jesus back

> *"I think so often as women we think that we have to do every-thing. Mary of Bethany is an example of a woman who decided to make a dent, to bring her action forward into a moment know-ing that it might not fix the situation, but giving it nonetheless."*
>
> **Elisa Morgan**

Small Group Study and Video Discussion

1. **Read:** Mark 14:1–9. We know from reading the story of Jesus' life in the Gospels that he cared deeply about the needs of the poor. What do you think Jesus is getting at when he affirms Mary's act of reckless generosity toward him and rebukes those who are critical of her?

2. Sometimes when we see the great needs of the world we are overwhelmed and start to wonder if our small contribution will really make much of a difference. What are some of the needs and problems you have encountered that seem overwhelming to you?

3. Elisa points out that Mary "lived *loved*." In other words, she had a profound and personal awareness of the truth that Jesus really loved her. Share a time in your journey of faith when you were overwhelmed by the reality that you are deeply and passionately loved by God. How does the awareness of God's love for you affect the way you serve others?

> "The gospel is living LOVED and acting out on our faith in the world."
>
> **Elisa Morgan**

4. "Mary did what she could." Her actions were in response to her awareness of Jesus' love for her and were an affirmation of her love for her Savior. In those moments when you are profoundly aware of God's love for you and of your own love for God, what acts of service come most naturally for you?

5. Mary did what she could; she acted. What are some things that can get in the way of you taking action to serve and honor God?

What is one action you know you need to take right now as Jesus' loved servant?

"Mary did what she could do!"

Elisa Morgan

6. Elisa says, "The gospel is our faith with feet on it." Who is one person you know who exemplifies putting feet on her faith? What is it about her life that inspires you?

7. Like Mary we are also called to take action to make a difference in our world. What are some possible steps your group can take together to show God's love in your church or community?

"When I do what I could, and you do what you could, and together we do what we could, like Mary of Bethany we love Jesus back, we put feet on our faith."

Elisa Morgan

8. Elisa tells a story about a time when she did *not* do what she could. She had overlooked the needs of a couple living right next door to her. Share about a time when you missed an opportunity to do what you could. What did you learn from this experience and how might it impact the way you respond to needs in the future?

9. What is the difference between doing "all we could" and "what we could"? Why does focusing on doing "all we could" often lead to feeling overwhelmed? How does committing to do "what we could" set us free?

10. Elisa talks about doing the "little things." Her examples were giving an hour to listen to a woman who was struggling, and laying with her grandson. Make a list of some different "little things" you could do in an ordinary day to show God's love and care to others.

Identify *one* of these that you could do in the coming forty-eight hours and share it with your group.

"*Mary got that Jesus loved her and that maybe the way to love him back was to serve, to put his love in her into action, to do what she could.*"

Elisa Morgan

Group Prayer Direction

◎ Thank Jesus that we can bring a blessing to him, that we can please him. Ask him to show you how to do that in ways that honor him.

◎ Pray for a growing hunger to be in the presence of Jesus.

◎ Confess those moments when you could have done what you could and made a difference, but you walked right past the opportunity.

◎ Pray for eyes to see and courage to respond the next time God gives you an opportunity to do what you can.

◎ Take the time to reflect on Psalm 27:4 and use its words to guide your prayers. "One thing I ask of the LORD, this is what I seek: that I may dwell in the house of the LORD all the days of my life, to gaze upon the beauty of the LORD and to seek him in his temple."

"The gospel is our faith with feet on it."

Elisa Morgan

Journal Between Sessions

Thank God for the people he has placed in your life who have made it a habit of doing what they could. Be specific about who these people are and how God has blessed your life through them. Consider thanking these people in person or by correspondence if possible.

Write down some of the ways God might use you to take action and do what you can to be a blessing to others. Again, be specific.

_____

_____

_____

_____

_____

_____

_____

_____

_____

_____

_____

_____

_____

_____

_____

MARTHA

FINDING OUR IDENTITY IN JESUS

Key Scripture:
Luke 10:38–42*

Amena Brown

* The timing of the events in Luke 10:38–42 is uncertain. Regardless of when the events in this passage occurred, the teaching and application of this passage remain the same—turning away from our distractions to focus on the one that really matters, Jesus.

MEETING MARTHA

*J*esus spent much of his time in the village of Bethany, where Martha, Mary, and Lazarus lived. Jesus loved this family and he had a deep friendship with all three siblings. Whenever he was visiting Bethany or traveling through, he would stay with them in their home.

As we saw in the last session, Martha's sister, Mary, was a woman of passion, motivated to act and serve by a deep devotion to Jesus. Yet of the two sisters, Mary was the more contemplative one, spending her time listening and learning at the feet of Jesus. Martha also loved to learn, but she was a woman of responsibility: a doer who loved to show her love through regular acts of service for others. While Mary showed her loved in extravagant, sacrificial devotion, Martha showed her love for Jesus in more routine ways: cooking, serving meals, and doing whatever she could to meet the practical needs of others. But as we learn through her questions of Jesus, Martha was also deeply spiritual and had a sharp theological mind! Martha understood the promise of the resurrection and she recognized that Jesus was the promised Messiah . . . something many of the most learned religious leaders were unwilling to accept or believe (see John 11:24–27).

Martha seems to have also felt comfortable confronting others and speaking her mind. After her brother Lazarus died, Martha confronted Jesus with a series of questions, expressing her pain and disappointment that Jesus had allowed her brother to die. And in yet another interaction, we learn that she felt comfortable reprimanding her sister for sitting and listening to Jesus while she was busy serving.

Jesus loved Martha and graciously responded to her honest concerns and questions. In particular, Jesus wanted Martha to understand that while her desire to serve was valuable and important, knowing God and being in his presence needed to take priority in her life. Her story and example should encourage us, inspiring us to keep serving, while reminding us that all God-honoring service must flow from a heart that is fully engaged with the Savior!

Introduction

Who are you? Where do you find your identity?

Many of us base our identity on certain roles and tasks that we do. And we evaluate our worth as a woman against how well we perform those tasks. We compare ourselves with others, judging our performance against theirs. If we are doing well relative to others, we feel good about ourselves—but if we aren't, we often feel like a failure.

Jesus was clear two thousand years ago that the true measure of a man or woman is not a matter of performing certain tasks or racking up a list of impressive accomplishments. Our value and identity are not based on what we have done (or will do), but on who we are in Jesus Christ. The most fundamental aspects of our identity are not what we accomplish and earn; they are the things we have been given. Our identity in Christ is a gift of God's grace, not a standing that we can earn by hard work and good intentions.

This is where Martha missed the mark. Though she had been touched by the love of Jesus, she still had moments when she was lured into believing the lie, thinking that her significance was found in doing the right things.

Cook great meals! Keep the house clean! Serve people! Accomplish stuff! That's what will make you loved and valued as a person.

But as honorable as these things can be, they are not our top priority in life. Jesus reminded Martha of a secret that is easily forgotten in the midst of our busy lives: our value, our worth, and our identity are not up for grabs every day based on how we behave or perform. They are locked securely in the heart of the God who loves us and gave his life for us.

Open your heart today and prepare to be set free as you discover your true identity in Jesus Christ, and in him alone!

Talk About It

Briefly respond as a group to one of the following questions.

What *was* a favorite room or space in your house when you were growing up and what made this space so special to you?

What *is* a favorite room or space in your home today and what makes this space so special to you?

"Jesus wants us to realize that we are never going to get our worth from what we do. There is only one place we are going to get our worth and that is from him."

Amena Brown

Video Teaching Notes

Martha's home and kitchen

Martha was a doer

Martha's story and frustration

Worrying versus trusting

The source of our identity and value

Jesus wants full access to all the places of your life

What are your "many things"?

Taking your "many things" to the feet of Jesus

Accept Jesus' invitation to be with God

> *"The more we are worried about our 'many things,' the more we show that we are not trusting in God."*
>
> **Amena Brown**

Small Group Study and Video Discussion

1. **Read:** Luke 10:38–42. What do we learn about Martha's heart from this passage? What do you think her question—"Lord, don't you care . . . ?"—reveals about the real source of her frustration?

2. As you look at Mary and Martha, which sister most reflects your natural way of doing life and how do you see yourself in this woman?

3. Sadly, when our lives get extra busy, the first thing to usually go is our time with Jesus. Take a few moments as a group to honestly talk about the pace of your life right now. Are you finding time and space to connect with God each day? If not, what is getting in the way?

4. Amena talks about Martha's natural desire to make everyone else happy, meeting the needs of others while her own heart is growing frustrated and discouraged. Describe a time when you saw this tendency in your own life. What are some of the dangers of trying to serve others this way?

"Martha is like some of us. We keep giving and giving and giving, but we are running on empty and surviving on fumes!"

Amena Brown

5. Jesus says to Martha, "You are worried and upset about many things." What are some of the "many things" that women today can get caught up worrying about?

In a normal week, what are some of the things you tend to worry and get upset about?

6. Amena suggests that sometimes we form our identity from what we do. What are some of the dangers of basing our sense of personal value on what we do and accomplish on a specific day? How does this contrast with the gospel and the identity we receive from God, by his grace?

7. Amena suggests thinking of ourselves as a house and imagining how some people have access to the porch, others are invited into the kitchen, and others have full run of the place. She then says Jesus wants full access to our house . . . our life. What area of your life are you tempted to hang a "Do Not Disturb" or "Stay Out" sign and try to keep Jesus away? Why is it important for Jesus to have full access to every area of our life and heart?

"Jesus wants the master key to your heart."

Amena Brown

8. Martha took her complaint directly to Jesus. She was honest, holding nothing back! What do you think about her honesty, and how could you be more like Martha in your communication with the Lord?

Group Prayer Direction

◎ Pray that you will make time to sit at the feet of Jesus and learn from him. Ask the Holy Spirit to make these times intimate and sweet.

◎ Ask God to help you trust him with your "many things."

◎ Bring the things you are "fussing over" to the throne of Jesus. Lay them down. Ask him to help you believe he can help you with all of these things.

◎ Confess that you can get busy and distracted and ask God to help you keep your focus on what matters most to him.

◎ Ask Jesus to help you live with such a deep awareness of his love that you are secure in who you are, because of who he is!

Journal Between Sessions

Martha was honest with Jesus. If you could be really honest with Jesus what would you say or ask him?

_____

_____

_____

_____

_____

_____

_____

_____

_____

_____

_____

_____

_____

_____

_____

_____

_____

_____

_____

THE WOMAN AT THE WELL

TURNING OUR MESSES
INTO MESSAGES

Key Scriptures: John 4:7–42
and Luke 17:11–19

Lysa TerKeurst

MEETING THE WOMAN AT THE WELL

*W*e never learn her name. She is simply called a *Samaritan* woman. But this amazing individual whom we meet in the fourth chapter of John's Gospel teaches us a deeply valuable lesson.

Three things are obvious, but very important to remember. First, she was a woman. In her world and time, this was one strike against her. Women were not trusted, invited into religious discourse, or even spoken to in public by rabbis. In addition to being a woman, she was also a Samaritan—strike two! The Jews looked down on the Samaritans because they had intermarried with the nations around them and were no longer "pure-blooded" enough to be considered true Jews. Finally, this Samaritan woman had a sinful past . . . and her present circumstances were questionable as well—strike three! We learn that she had been married and divorced *five* times and was now living with a man who was not her husband.

Reading the story even more closely, we can infer some additional details about the woman. For instance, there is a good chance this woman was poor. Those who had money usually sent someone else to draw their water for them, but this woman had to draw her own from the well. She obviously couldn't afford to pay someone else. In addition, the time of her arrival at the well suggests that she was most likely a social outcast. Most women would come to draw water early in the day, while it was still cool. But the woman in our story comes in the heat of the day, likely to avoid the gossip and accusing stares of the women from town.

Surprisingly, we also discover that the woman of our story had a sharp theological mind and was open to talking about spiritual matters. Though she did not fully understand everything Jesus said to her, she was hungry to learn and had obviously spent some time thinking about what she believed. Her encounter with Jesus at the well completely transformed her understanding of God, as she came to believe that Jesus was the long-awaited Messiah . . . the Savior of the world.

The encounter with Jesus at the well not only changed the Samaritan woman's life. Immediately, she began to share what she had found with everyone she knew.

Introduction

In one sense, the encounter between Jesus and the Samaritan woman at the well is not all that unique. It's an encounter that has been repeated again and again throughout the ages.

We meet a woman whose life is in shambles, fragmented and broken by sin. Her life is a real mess. While drawing water from the local well, she meets the Messiah. They talk, she asks questions, and something wonderful happens. Her eyes are opened to the truth, her heart is touched by the kindness of Jesus, and she is transformed by God's power. A whole new life begins for her. In John, chapter four, we witness this metamorphosis: a woman whose life is a profound mess, an outcast from the community, becomes the bearer of a life-giving message to the very people she had been avoiding. *Her mess became her message when she met the Messiah!*

What God did in and through this woman two thousand years ago can become the anthem of your life as well. Romans 5:8 tells us that "God demonstrates his own love for us in this: While we were still sinners, Christ died for us." God knows our frailties, our wrong attitudes, and is aware of each of our sins. Yet he still loves us, and he wants to fill us and use us for his glory. When we bring our mess to the Messiah, he restores us and gives us a message for the world.

As you prepare for this study, be open and ready for God to speak. God just might be calling you to be his messenger in a new and fresh way!

Talk About It

Briefly respond as a group to one of the following questions.

Sometimes we have one of those really good days, the kind we wish could go on and on forever. Talk about a "good day" you experienced recently and what made that day so special for you!

Some days are just plain messy! Things spin out of control and we need someone to help us clean up. Talk about a day you've had when things in your life got a bit messy.

Video Teaching Notes

The story of the Samaritan woman at the well

No quick answers, convenient solutions, and easy fixes

This woman has a divine encounter with Jesus

Jesus wants to deal with your messes and give you a message

Lysa's story: Jesus' divine encounter

Jesus, the Messiah, is the perfect fit for our mess, and he will give us a message of hope

The story of ten lepers

Jesus heals and restores

Where are you in this story?

"The first four letters of the word 'Messiah' is mess. It is almost as if Jesus, the Messiah, is the perfect fit for our mess. God knew we would have a mess and that the Messiah would come and touch our mess and out of that, would give us a message."

Lysa TerKeurst

Small Group Study and Video Discussion

1. **Read:** John 4:4–15. Jesus had a deep and thoughtful conversation with this woman at the well. (This is extraordinary: Jewish rabbis in the first century never talked about faith, the Scriptures, or theology with women.) What were some of the topics Jesus and the woman conversed about? How did these topics connect the heart of this woman with the heart of God in new ways?

2. Often, when Jesus had a conversation with a person, his words would have meaning on a deeper, more spiritual level, yet the other person would still be thinking at a more concrete and literal level. How do you see this happening in this interaction? Where do you see Jesus and the woman using the same words but talking about different things?

3. Look closely at Jesus' treatment of this outcast woman. What does his example teach us about how we should treat those outside of faith and on the margins of society?

4. What was the Samaritan woman's "mess" and how did Jesus clean it up?

5. What are some of the shallow answers and quick fixes that Christians sometimes deliver to people who are in the midst of a tough and messy time? What are the dangers of such simplistic, canned answers?

"Jesus says that he gives answers but they are not going to be shallow, and he give fixes but they are not going to be quick."

Lysa TerKeurst

6. **Read:** John 4:16–42. Lysa observes that the woman at the well likely wants quick and convenient answers to solve her temporary problems. At first, she is not looking for the deeper spiritual solutions Jesus offers to her. How do you see this attitude in people today? How have you seen this attitude filter into your own life?

7. How has God entered a messy situation or time of your life and, with his grace and power, turned it into a message?

"Each time I share how God takes my mess and uses it for good, I am not only cleansed, I am not only healed, I am made completely well as if I had never had that mess in the first place."

Lysa TerKeurst

8. **Read:** Luke 17:11–19. What do we learn about the power of Jesus to clean up messes and the place of thankfulness in this passage?

What are some things you are grateful to God for today?

"Your mess can be touched by the Messiah and you can have a message of hope and redemption."

Lysa TerKeurst

Group Prayer Direction

◎ Pray for God to reveal any way you marginalize or avoid people and ask the Holy Spirit to give you power and courage to reach out to these people with the living water of Jesus.

◎ Confess where you have messes in your life and ask Jesus, the Messiah, to help clean them up.

◎ Ask God to give you a clear and powerful message to share with others and invite the Spirit of God to inspire you and prompt you to share this message at the right times.

◎ Pray that your local church will be a place that accepts and embraces people, even with their messes. Ask God to shape your church into a place that encourages people to come as they are, and walks with them as they become all God wants them to be.

◎ Ask God to help you throw away the false things you use to satisfy yourself. Pray that you will thirst more and more for the water of life that only Jesus can bring.

Journal Between Sessions

Jesus' encounter with the woman teaches us about social relationships and how we sometimes avoid and ignore people of certain standings. Journal about your own life and ask God to reveal any groups of people you might avoid, ignore, or marginalize.

_____

_____

_____

_____

_____

_____

_____

_____

_____

_____

_____

_____

_____

_____

_____

_____

_____

_____

THE SYROPHOENICIAN WOMAN

APPROACHING GOD WITH PERSISTENCY AND BOLDNESS

Key Scriptures: Matthew 15:21–28 and Mark 7:26

Naomi Zacharias

MEETING THE SYROPHOENICIAN WOMAN

*T*he woman we encounter in today's session could easily be defined by all that she was *not* . . .

She was *not* Jewish, she was a *Gentile*. In first-century Palestine the Jewish people divided the entire world into two groups: Jews and non-Jews (Gentiles). She would have been despised by the Jewish people; some may have even called her a "Gentile dog" or another derogatory name. But in a world where Jews and Gentiles did not have a great deal of social interaction (or respect for one another), this woman broke through the cultural barriers that separated her from Jesus and brought her heartfelt requests directly to him.

She was *not* a local girl; to meet with Jesus she had to come from the "other side of the tracks" into a different part of town. But she wasn't just a nameless, faceless, pawn in the biblical narrative. We learn that she was a concerned and loving *mother*. This was a real woman, with real hopes, real dreams, and a real family. And she had a little girl who was being tormented by a demon. Like any good mother, she wanted relief for her child.

Finally, she was *not* passive and submissive as women were often expected to be. Instead, she was *passionate* and *driven*. This woman had faith that Jesus could deliver her precious little girl from her affliction and she was not going to settle for anything less than the best for her daughter. She was ready to plead with the disciples, with Jesus, and with heaven itself for deliverance. We learn that she appeals to Jesus not once or twice, but three times! Her passion to see her daughter restored and healed drove her to relentlessly pursue the only one who could set the child free . . . Jesus.

Despite the list of "nots" that defined her life, the woman of our story had something that Jesus commended: *faith*. Her faith was in the person and power of Jesus. And at a time when many of those who surrounded Jesus failed to grasp who he was, this Gentile woman demonstrates amazing insight, calling him "Lord" and the "Son of David." She believed that he could perform a miracle.

The next time you are tempted to define someone by what they are *not*, pause and remember this woman. Take time to dig a little deeper—beyond the surface judgments and stereotypes—and discover who they really are in the eyes of God.

Introduction

Sometimes we get the impression that the Bible teaches women to be quiet, submissive, and reserved. And while there are certainly passages of Scripture that praise these attributes, there is more to the biblical definition of a woman. The Word of God also gives us snapshots of women who were bold, strong, and tenacious in their pursuit of Jesus—and were commended for that. The Canaanite woman in this story is a model of unyielding persistence and passionate prayer. She cried out to Jesus, over and over, until her daughter was delivered—a dynamic story of confident intercession!

Sometimes we wrongly assume that Jesus responded to every request with predictable tenderness and immediate concern. But in this story we see a different pattern. Jesus seems somewhat resistant, even uninterested and a bit harsh, toward this hurting woman. Yet there is more happening here than meets the eye. The tender love of Jesus is still present, but he is teaching something new through his actions. Though he is going to eventually heal the daughter of this Gentile woman, he wants to use this opportunity to teach his disciples (and us today) a much bigger lesson.

In this passage we discover numerous lessons for our lives today, but we need to dig a little deeper to find them. As you study this woman and her encounter with Jesus, be prepared to learn about the sovereign power of God over time and space, the love of God for all people of all places, and the complexity of how Jesus interacts with people. Things are not always what they appear to be at first glance. Take some time with this passage, study deeply, and you will discover the rich and textured truth about Jesus.

Talk About It

Briefly respond as a group to one of the following questions.

Talk about a portion of the Bible or a particular Bible story that you had a hard time understanding when you first studied it.

Share with the group about a time when you felt rejected, left out, or forgotten.

"It is one thing to believe someone can do something. It is an entirely different thing to believe with confidence that they will!"

Naomi Zacharias

Video Teaching Notes

The story of the woman approaching Jesus

Three questions that arise in this passage

Understanding how the Jews viewed Gentiles in the first century

The significance of the text "they glorified the God of Israel"

Understanding what Jesus meant by the word "dog"

How the disciples were tested in this encounter

The woman's persistence and how her outlook changed as she encountered Jesus

Our struggle for identity and significance as women

Jesus Christ is the answer

"All of our answers rest in Jesus alone."

Naomi Zacharias

Small Group Study and Video Discussion

1. **Read:** Matthew 15:21–28 and Mark 7:26. Naomi points out that this story takes place outside of Jewish territory and that Jesus had gone there to connect with people who were not followers of the faith. What are some of the places and settings today where we can encounter people who are far from Jesus and in need of his love and grace? What can Christians do to engage with people in these kinds of places?

2. What message did Jesus send to the Jews (including his disciples) when he started healing Gentiles? What message was Jesus sending to the Gentiles through his inclusion of them in his healing ministry?

3. When the disciples saw the woman coming to Jesus, they encouraged him to send her away, not wanting him to be "bothered." What do you think was going on in their hearts, and how have you seen the modern church and Christians send people away or ignore those who are in need? What can we do to make sure we don't have the same exclusive attitude as the disciples?

4. The woman in this story comes and confidently asks of Jesus, believing that he is willing and able to answer her prayer and grant her request. What can we do to pray and seek the face of Jesus with greater passion and persistence?

"The woman began by making a request and ended with a prayer to the one she believed in."

Naomi Zacharias

5. Naomi points out that the woman in this story asks for Jesus' help three times, persistent in her belief that he will grant her request. In the end, we learn that she is right; she receives from Jesus what she asks. Tell about a time when God answered a prayer that you lifted up persistently and over a long period of time. What kept you praying even when time seemed to drag on?

> "This woman comes to Jesus knowing that she has nothing, she does not feel like she deserves anything, there is no sense of entitlement, and she realizes how small she is. But she also realizes that Jesus has exactly what she needs and she is confident that he will give it to her."
>
> **Naomi Zacharias**

6. Naomi talks about how Jesus often did not give simple answers, but left things vague, making room for people to discover and learn deeper things about him. Why do you think Jesus does this?

7. Even when someone tells us the truth, we may not fully grasp it at first. What are some aspects of knowing and following Jesus that have taken time for you to understand?

> *"This woman believes that a crumb from Jesus is actually an entire feast for her."*
>
> **Naomi Zacharias**

8. Sometimes we are tempted to rest secure at our own place at the table with Jesus and ignore the needs and struggles of others. Like the disciples, we may be tempted to brush other people away as bothersome distractions. How have you experienced this, and what can you do to make sure these kinds of attitudes and actions are not part of your life patterns?

> *"There is neither Jew nor Greek, neither slave nor free, nor is there male and female, for you are all one in Christ Jesus."*
>
> **Galatians 3:28**

Group Prayer Direction

◎ Praise God that he has the power to deliver us (and those we love) from evil.

◎ Ask God to give you a persistency in pursuing him as you bring the needs and concerns of others to Jesus.

◎ Lift your most urgent requests and needs for others and for yourself before the one who cares and is listening.

◎ Thank Jesus for his sovereign power over space and time. Praise him that he can heal, deliver, and provide with a simple word.

◎ Pray for a heart and attitude that wants others to come to Jesus . . . no matter what their history. Ask the Holy Spirit to give you a tender heart and to protect you from the temptation to look past certain groups or types of people.

Journal in the Coming Days

Near the end of the conversation, the Syrophoenician woman calls Jesus "Lord." It appears she shifts from a focus on what Jesus could do for her to who he was. The prayer life of many Christians focuses primarily on what Jesus can do for them. It's all about making requests. While there is nothing wrong with this, there is more to prayer than simple requests. As we mature in faith, we discover the wonder of adoration and worship . . . praising God for who he is! Journal about several attributes or qualities of God that you celebrate, reflecting on how you have experienced God in these different ways.

SMALL GROUP LEADER HELPS

To ensure a successful small group experience, read the following information before beginning.

Group Preparation

Whether your small group has been meeting together for years or is gathering for the first time, be sure to designate a consistent time and place to work through the twelve sessions. Once you establish the when and where of your times together, select a facilitator who will keep discussions on track and an eye on the clock. If you choose to rotate this responsibility, assign the twelve sessions to their respective facilitators up front, so that they can prepare their thoughts and questions prior to the session they are responsible for leading. Follow the same assignment procedure should your group want to serve any snacks/beverages.

A Note to Facilitators

As facilitator, you are responsible for honoring the agreed-upon timeframe of each meeting, for prompting helpful discussion among your group, and for keeping the dialogue equitable by drawing out quieter members and helping more talkative participants to remember that others' insights are also valued in your group.

You might find it helpful to preview each session's video teaching segment and then scan the "Small Group Study and Video Discussion" questions that pertain to it, highlighting various questions that you want to be sure to cover during your group's meeting. Before your group meets, ask God to guide the discussion, and then be sensitive to the direction in which he wishes to lead.

Session Format

Each session of the participant's guide includes the following group components:

- **"Introduction"**—an entrée to the session's featured Bible woman/theme, which may be read by a volunteer or summarized by the facilitator
- **"Talk About It"**—a choice of icebreaker questions that relates to the session topic and invites input from every group member
- **"Video Teaching Notes"**—an outline of the session's video teaching for group members to follow along and take notes if they wish

- **"Small Group Study and Video Discussion"**—Bible exploration and questions that reinforce the session content and elicit personal input from every group member; interspersed throughout are featured quotations from the video teacher or key Bible verses
- **"Group Prayer Direction"**—several cues related to the session themes to guide group members in closing prayer

Additionally, in each session you will find a helpful one-page "Meeting . . ." biography on the featured Bible woman as well as a guided "Journal Between Sessions" section that allows group members to reflect on the session themes more deeply between meetings.

Personal Preparation

Practically, you'll want to bring the following items to each group meeting:

- Your Bible
- This participant's guide and a pen
- The video and a device on which to play/display it

Enjoy your time together!

ABOUT THE PRESENTERS

Lysa TerKeurst is the #1 *New York Times* bestselling author of *Uninvited, The Best Yes,* and several other books and video studies. She is president of Proverbs 31 Ministries and writes from her sticky farm table in North Carolina. She still has a crush on her husband, Art, who she's been married to for twenty-four years. They deeply treasure every minute they can get with their four married kids and one teenager who still keeps them very young. Connect with her at www.LysaTerKeurst.com.

Jeanne Stevens is one of the lead pastors of Soul City Church in the dynamic West Loop neighborhood of Chicago, Illinois. Prior to starting Soul City Church in 2010, Jeanne served on the staff of Willow Creek Community Church for eleven years as a student ministry pastor and on the staff of North Point Community Church for four years. She is also the author of *Soul School.* Connect with her at www.jeannestevens.com.

Jonalyn Grace Fincher is the author of *Ruby Slippers: How the Soul of a Woman Brings Her Home* and is one half of Soulation (www.soulation.org), a husband/wife teaching team. She holds a master's degree in philosophy of religion and ethics from Talbot School of Theology, as well as double bachelor's degrees in English and history from the University of Virginia. While at seminary at Biola University's Talbot School of Theology, she met and married Dale Fincher. After a year teaching junior high, Dale and Jonalyn joined forces and founded Soulation, a nonprofit dedicated to helping people become more fully human. They live in the Rocky Mountains.

Amena Brown is a poet, speaker, author, and event host. She is the author of *Breaking Old Rhythms* and a spoken word CD "Live at Java Monkey." Amena has performed and spoken at events across the nation such as The RightNow Conference, Creativity World Forum, Catalyst Conference, Leadercast, as well as touring with Gungor. She and her husband, Matt, also known as DJ Opdiggy, travel and perform a presentation of poetry, monologue, and deejaying. They also host a regular open mic in Atlanta every fifth Thursday at Urban Grind Coffee. Connect with her at www.amenabrown.com.

Elisa Morgan was named by *Christianity Today* as one of the top fifty women influencing today's church and culture and is one of today's most sought-after authors, speakers, and leaders. She has authored over twenty-five books on mothering, spiritual formation, and evangelism, including *Hello, Beauty Full*, *The Beauty of Broken*, *She Did What She Could: Five Words of Jesus That Will Change Your Life*, the *NIV Mom's Devotional Bible*. For twenty years, Elisa Morgan served as CEO of MOPS International (www.mops.org). She now serves MOPS as President Emerita. Connect with her at www.elisamorgan.com.

Naomi Zacharias serves as the director of Wellspring International, the humanitarian initiative of Ravi Zacharias International Ministries. From the red-light districts of Amsterdam, Bombay, and Bangkok, to children's HIV/AIDS foster homes and women's prisons in South Africa, Naomi works to provide funding for rescue, rehabilitation, education, and support for women and children throughout the world. She is the author of *A Scent of Water: Grace for Every Kind of Broken* and now lives in Atlanta, Georgia with her husband, Drew. Connect with her at www.naomizacharias.com.

ABOUT THE WRITER

Sherry Harney is an author and speaker for national and international groups. She serves as the leadership development director at Shoreline Community Church in Monterey, California. She is also the cofounder, along with her husband Kevin, of Organic Outreach International, a ministry that trains church and movement leaders to mobilize their members to go into their community and world and naturally share the good news of Jesus. Over the past twenty-five years Sherry has cowritten and collaborated on over seventy small group studies with such authors as Ann Voskamp, Christine Caine, Max Lucado, Nabeel Qureshi, Bill Hybels, John Ortberg, Mark Batterson, Gary Thomas, and Dallas Willard. Sherry and Kevin have three adult sons and two daughter-in-laws. Sherry loves to hike, ski, read, cook, and hang out with family and friends. She is passionate about living her life with Jesus, like Jesus, and for Jesus.

Twelve More Women of the Bible Study Guide with DVD

Life-Changing Stories for Women Today

Karen Ehman, Lisa Harper, Margaret Feinberg, Bianca Juárez Olthoff, Chrystal Evans Hurst, Courtney Joseph

In this 12-session video Bible study, some of today's best-loved authors and speakers look at the spiritual lessons learned from twelve women in the Bible and what they mean for you today. As you look at each of these women's lives, you will discover how to:

- Apply biblical lessons to your own modern-day struggles
- Live through your failures as well as your successes
- Draw near to God in a world filled with trials
- Find lasting contentment in every situation
- Overcome rejection and insecurity and much more

This fresh look at these women in the Bible will help you discover new insights into God's character, persevere through difficult times, and find joy in the hope that Jesus has provided to you. The study guide, by Sherry Harney, includes background information on each woman, group discussion questions, Bible exploration, and personal study and reflection materials for in-between sessions.

Sessions include:

1. Proverbs 31 Woman: How Not to Do It All
2. Deborah: Fight Like a Girl
3. Shulamite Woman: We Had God at Hello
4. Ruth: Staying Focused in a World of Distractions
5. Puah and Shiprah: How to Fight Your Fears
6. Esther: Letting God Be in Control
7. Priscilla: Living a Life of Blessed Ordinary
8. Mary and Martha: Finding Life in Death
9. Bent Woman: We've Got God's Complete Attention
10. Woman with the Issue of Blood: When Persistence Pays Off
11. Elizabeth: How to Win the Waiting Game
12. Anna: How to Live a Life Devoted to God

Available in stores and online!